even gods

allyson jeffredo

Copyright @ 2021 by Allyson Jeffredo
ISBN: 978-1-7332415-9-5
Published by Jamii Publishing
San Bernadino, CA
www.JamiiPublishing.com
All rights reserved.

"Perhaps he'd turn into a god and they to trees."
—Cormac McCarthy, *The Road*

"¿Para qué sufrir si no hace falta?"
—Natalia Lafourcade, "Para Qué Sufrir"

contents

there is power	7
we turn into gods	8
against all	9
there was a song	10
the mother dreamed of water	11
we weren't broken	12
of love in our gut	13
in our depths	14
perhaps we'd turn	15
maybe we	18
we were gods	19
a holiness	20
the first time we died	21
if our feet met	22
our trouble is	23
doesn't make tragic	24
will hold us	25
us gods	28
the mother, perhaps only	29
making gods	30

there is power behind these letters — *no*
a whisper, a command — sketch us as
small gods or giants or mothers
each time she asks the weather
to act right, it doesn't listen, but no
one laughs, we turn into gods
behind her back, still in her image
god only makes sense as a woman
with her back pressed against brick
her arm, her hip left burned — even gods are damaged

perhaps

we turn into gods as cars
idle aside a busy road—we're there
and not there, passersby pretend they're us
for a moment, finding magic
as they envision our dashboard full of dog hair
and left-over pizza boxes. there
is an apotheosis in the jump
there is power in accepting we
are what make up the forgotten
behind someone's breath, a re-member:

against all my better judgment
i believe in ghosts and their power
to find us//wherever we go—

there was a song,
a hum low in our chests
a break through
the sternum, a block
in its way, but if it can escape
our voice finds the float
the dream of mothhood

fluttering in the somewhere

the mother dreamed of water
but it was a mirage, a pool
lined by the sun—her thirst
so hard to quench

in the desert
                      she's a ghost, a god, a hand
                      directing
those thirsty for shade
or a path to holiness
where wind comes
to claim the only
water we have to give

our ears at the door
our breath hard in our chests

we weren't broken until someone said

there's our feet in the living room
our hair caught in the santa anas
our breath between door splinters

wholeness a scurry of pieces

our hands cut from their wrists
the distance between our fingers
a short inch from tip to tip

in the tedious space of just

when we see the sun, we hear whispers
of love in our gut, where
sadness is only water spots

air breaks
across our face and we find ourselves
in the impact. our throats
seize, we pull the choke
from its depths — revealing im-
mortality is the soft, calloused palms
of another, the drift of sand over
cement. in this circle, the bountiful
edges of belong & shame
find its way into this cold
today is ours for the let-go

perhaps we'd turn into sound
if we learned how to let go, how
do i say there is no sound
for love, there is no shape
for sorry, there is only

maybe this we
always and never was
you
&
i
an us
unable to find
our way out or
back in

we
were gods
in a bathroom stall
forming and unforming words
hard upon the tongue
our bodies merging into
walls, relics of hands
& footprints imprinted
of oil & water, transcriptions
britney was here / who cares?
scratched into our bodies
a plea for permanence
within this quivering shape

there is a holiness
in the shadows of any
wholly worn place

the first time we died
we were found in the gutter
we were wasps in a flood
trapped asunder the sun
a toast, a mourning
between too many
& not enough

perhaps we turned into gods
when our feet met in the dark

                                    we beat
to the world's breath
& she sleeps better at night
knowing this shape
turns us human

what were we before we met?

paper edges, eggshells, glass shards

taking up space instead of making it
an atlas, our bodies finding the walls
this room is ours & never left us

we are the room dressed in color
someone wants to wash over
but here we are with feet together

dreaming

your face in my hands yellow
from the sun kiss against your brow
the dimples of scars along your cheeks

this *we* might not be meant
to keep but meant it is
or meant it was
or meant it should be

perhaps   our trouble
is living, i
indeed that
      darkness
the loss   a moment
to see   or dream
a man—
      a dream
             of once

i love
i insist
i think
i consider
i have
i want

the face   the love
      however
the face   the baby
a   part
          agony
brings
her head   under
a wind
the bottom
        the bury
a room
      aflame
take care
      of the after
is far too tragic
            or was

perhaps living under this sun
perhaps breathing or gasping
perhaps lying or colding
perhaps opening or closing
perhaps

        doesn't passion
        doesn't hold
        doesn't sulk
        doesn't beauty
        doesn't make
                      tragic

if this were a tragedy,

who would hold us in the quiet?

who would hold us through the fracture?

who would breathe breath into our dry frames?

who will
will who
who?

there is a song in the sun:

us gods, us forgiveness
us pettiness, us hollow
us glasses, us granite
us harrow, us follow
us tables, us pictures
us you, us me, us i
us she, us keep, us he
us hard, us deep
us more, us short
us, take my hand

no, please, let it go

the mother, perhaps only a god
holds a picture in her hands
we pass it between us to break the space
it's not hubble-worthy but she insists
there is a god between her fingers
we watch her cross herself
as if she'll hold onto this god forever

in this apotheosis
we cry. making gods of particles
the transformation more for us
then them, we cry
holding the god, the mother
because what would we be
without the other

www.ingramcontent.com/pod-product-compliance
Lightning Source LLC
Chambersburg PA
CBHW040003110526
44587CB00001BA/37